ALLOWING NOW

A BOOK OF MINDFULNESS POETRY

ORNA ROSS

FontPublications

INTRODUCTION

MINDFULNESS POETRY FOR CREATIVE PRESENCE

This is a book of mindfulness poetry. Some, like the title poem, "Allowing Now", address the topic head on, some explore related themes like acceptance, inter-being and letting go.

Though we've only recently started to use this word for it, poets—and poetry readers—have always cultivated the truth, magic and mystery that are the heart of mindfulness.

When we move more deeply into the moment we're in, we move into a state of creative presence. Dormant faculties waken. Insight, imagination, intuition, inspiration are all magnified. We see more, perceive more, know more.

The sensory details of that moment, and its meaning for the poet, are experienced by the senses and later, in another deep moment, expressed in words. Then the sense and sound, rhythm and rhyme of those words, somehow transmit that moment, and its interpretation, to the reader.

It's a miracle of recreation, the profoundest possible homage to the miracle of creation itself.

The greatest gift readers can offer a poet is their own creative presence, the ability to stop their thoughts for a time, to listen deeply. Then poetry can happen in the reading, as it did in the writing.

In a mindful reading, the poem is like a soft white cloud, or a darker grey cloud, on the big, open, blue sky of the mind.

White cloud or grey, we don't judge. It's not about whether we like the poem or don't like it, whether it is better or worse than another poem. It's about listening.

Listening not just with the ears but with the whole body. Listening not just for the words but also for the spaces between the words that carry the poem's full meaning.

A good poet brings everything, a whole life, to the object or experience being written up. And a good reader brings everything, a whole life, to the reading.

INSTRUCTIONS FOR MINDFUL READING

- Find a place where you won't be disturbed for a little while and sit in a comfortable way. Add cushions, blankets, candles, anything that adds to your comfort. Then relax.
- Connect to the fact that you are breathing. Don't change your breath in any way, just notice it. Stay connected, brain to breath, for a few moments.
- Now open the page, and read the words silently or aloud.
- Notice if your mind wanders, gently bring it back to the words on the page.
- When you are finished the poem, sit still. Don't move away. Don't rush to read another one. Don't analyse. Don't judge. Just let it reverberate, like the sounding of a bell, within you.
- Connect to your breath again.
- Read the poem again.

A mindful poem mindfully read dissolves confusion and encourages clarity, dissolves anxiety and encourages peace, dissolves distraction

2

and encourages focus. It provides a refuge within which to recharge and reconnect with the truth of life.

I hope that you'll enjoy listening to and reading these poems aloud, copying lines into your f-r-e-e-writing notebook or journal, passing them onto friends. This, to me, is the highest praise, dearer than any glowing review or prestigious award.

I hope too that this book will encourage you to read more mindful and inspirational poetry and to re-read. Poems have a life, just as you do. They will change with you.

May your life be filled with poetry!

x Orna

PRESENCE

GOOD MORNING

The light of the sun
is spreading
over the sea
across the fields
down by the rivers
around the town,

creeping
into the cracks in rocks
the veins in leaves
the pores in skin,

sliding
under the slits
in the lids of eyes

tugging
at sinews in its silent
insistent way
to say:

Wake up.
Come out
of your lying
and sleeping.

I am here: a new day.
A new day.
A new day.

DAY OUT AT GLENDALOUGH

After you have walked the ruins
of seven churches,
tilted back your head to seek the top
of the tower that took
the rounded point
of Kevin's steeple
and thrust it up,
three times as high,
from earth to sky to mark
the ground you walk upon
as holy;

after you have circled green lake paths
that urge you up, then further up,
to top the crashing
waterfall, then
higher;

after you've been stopped and stopped again,
by sight of ice-sliced mountain cut to valley
its mesh of rivers and falls,

rushing to empty all into two, long lakes
that somehow take this ceaseless gush
and hold it
still,

you will know
the allure of here,
as of all the places we call sacred,
is the silence.

You will have heard
the voice
of your own blood
dropping into
the deep.

MOONWALKING

I half-walk, half-jog through silver-bright night
light, over pavement cracks, past frosted trees
and garden lawns—our sleeping suburb—
towards the park. I turn a corner,
am apprehended by the moon

which seems to have dropped to earth,
showing something of her true expanse,
and the glow she borrows from the sun, glosses
silver and makes her own, was surely never
brighter than on this winter morning
night, as she hovers just above, seeming to eye
me, face to face, a dazzle and delight.

Later I will learn how,
while I slept
she was eclipsed (again)
but this time she showed
blood (and how such
an event comes rarer
than a century's turn)

Now, as our city
wakens under the silver
sheet wrapped round it
in dead of night, and
starts to stir
into its morning
imperative, I am still.

Held in place by her, blood moon,
blue moon, super-moon as,
eclipse passed, she shines out
her heart for us. For me, for the trees,
for the grass beneath: we're all aglow,
the color of a spider's web after rain,
of sea foam as it fades into the sand,
of the gleam you sometimes see in
the eye of a child, that knowledge
of something we can almost forget
as we grow into our fullness.

Now we stand reminded,
breathing in moonshine, awed
and illuminated, swaddled within
bright night and dawning day.

TEN HAIKU

MOMENTS OF CREATIVE PRESENCE

Most days I write a haiku or two as a method of generating creative presence (See my book *How to Write Haiku*).

Haiku is a popular Japanese poetic form used to describe creative moments, often in #nature, through three short lines arranged in a fixed number of syllables. #575 is a common variant; I prefer #373.

I post my haiku on my Instagram page @ornaross using the hashtag: #creativemoments. Join me there?

HAIKU I

at sundown
one leaf reflecting the light
of the world

HAIKU II

lake water
bird in stillness standing
not waiting

HAIKU III

above a dry
riverbed trees whisper the
sound of water

HAIKU IV

when we first
meet we walk shy hands held
in our pockets

HAIKU V

after you leave
under my boots on dry grass
leaves crackle

HAIKU VI

evening lake
holds a great house a grey sky
shimmering

HAIKU VII

in the woods
startled by a startled bird
flaring into flight

HAIKU VIII

as I pass
he holds out a rose flower
smell and sweat

HAIKU IX

a flower
stalk standing still in water
leaves fallen

HAIKU X

above dark
clouds moon shines its path of light
on water

SEE YOU ON INSTAGRAM?

Join me on Instagram (Instagram.com/ornaross)
and share your own #creativemoments
in #haiku?

RAINBOW

After you leave
what do I spy
by gift of rain-
fractured light,
over the houses
between the trees
beyond the clouds,
but seven strips
of color
in an upside-
down smile,
traversing the sky?

COMING TO

On my back in the dark.
given up to night, I lie,
a fool aground. A suckling.
yearning, turning in want
and will, smothering
in the urges
of the underneath.

Up there
the spangled stars.
The moon: one-quarter lit
and on the wane.
Hiding its hollows
in its divide.
And the black
beyond.
That dark
that shades
the darkness.
That lacuna.

Night pulls me in

Night pulls me in
Night holds me still.
Night holds my wants
against my will,
until I am upended,
released to rise
again.

Oh stars, shining in from forever
ago, unfathomable in your million
millions (Why so many?) And
in your age. (*How* old?).
Your hearts exploding
into dust
somehow making us?

Oh moon, so cratered and so constant.
Growing darkness in the month's
declining shine, showing all fullness
shades to fading. Then back again.

Oh dear darkness
that sets all
the light alight.
Oh yes, our dear
goodnight.

Held, I hold.

Until
I take all in
again.

The milky ways of silken stars;
the mingled shades of ink between;

the black and blue; the human moon.

And all I've said and felt and seen.
All here. All held. All level held.

All level and forever held. Here,
in my own holding, in the empyrean.

SALEMA MOODS

OCEAN PULSE

SALEMA MOODS I

Rising, curling, foam unfurling,
waves of cold Salema sea.

Next one coming, meet it running,
plunge into the safe beneath,

Avoiding crashing, hard sand-smashing
sure to knock me to my knees.

Waves keep surging, endless burgeon
thrown up from the darkest deep.

Out here holding, look I'm floating,
blood-beat drumming in my ears,

surface splaying, breath delaying,
face bathed in your mystery
that's always saying all to me.

HERE IS WHERE

SALEMA MOODS II

I've been here
before but
now I'm here
for healing.

Twice times ill
with cancer
and its cure
here is where
I've come. Numb
beyond - or
should I say
beneath? - these,
my extremities,

I've been here
before, but
now I'm here
for healing.

SEEING EYE

SALEMA MOODS III

I'm rocked in salt arms: the ocean,
waves pillowing under my head.

The sky's eye seems to wink open
to glint all I seek to reflect.

For one glittering, infinite instant
I can't tell the fall from the swell.

THE RINGS OF OUR BEING

My love, and my hope,
from here will we go
into the wood
down by the river,
scattering the dew
of this day.

There we'll see the trout
and the bulrushes,
the blackbird on its nest,
the little birds
that are sweetest
singing in twos
from their branches.

I do not ask today
for your love as duty.
I shall not cling
and you'll not be
my strangulation.

I ask only to walk,
and sometimes to run,
to sit and lie down with you
under the kindness of trees.

There will we meet
the shy deer,
and the buck calling.

When you trip,
I'll help you to your feet.

Will you wait for me,
when someday I run slow?

Let us be together
without having or holding

And may we never bring in
the idea of making
the other better.

I am not your task.
You are already complete.

Only let the rings
of your being
widen in mine,
mine in yours.

Then death
shall never devour us.

For as long as we live
will we thrive
down by the river
in the dew-dappled wood.

A STANDING STONE IN GLADSTONE PARK

Longer than forever ago there lived
a people whom we, squinting
back through thickets of time,
like to call The Celts. It's said
they worshipped trees,
as ancient people widely did,
as any soulful person must,

and where I come from,
(an island off an island off
the continental shelf of Europe,
a little place a long time
on the outer edge of things)
some of the Celtic ways,
if that is what they were, lasted,
through centuries of stones
and spears, monks
and mothers, mansions,
cottages and bombs, dark
ages and enlightenments, all
the way to our own time.

So I grew up with Cold War
and central heating, nuclear
threat and hippie love, yet still
knowing holy wells, fairy forts, banshees,
Lughnasa and Bealtaine,
the real meaning of Halloween.

And then, this morning, on my park run
through my city park, where I live now,
(a metropolis a long time at the heart of things)
I saw a circle of trees, planted in what they say
was the Celtic way to make a sacred grove,
and marked by what is, unmistakably,
a miniature standing stone.

I stepped into the circle, circled
the upright stone, and, full of wonder,
wondered: Who made this?
Which park worker by stealth, or
council boss by stroke of pen,
decreed that it would be?

Well, here it is.
The trees are thriving and
the stone attracts scratchers
with sharp instruments
to pen magic eyes
and declarations of everlasting love.
I've come back to stand beside it now,
an hour from sunset, to lean against it
into the glow of a day not quite over.

And as I do, I know the stone
and all it stands for. Like its big siblings
Stonehenge. Newgrange, the pyramids,
it will outlast us, outlast probably
the knowledge of us.

As the sun sets in Gladstone Park,
this silent outcrop of an ancient way
of worship holds the rush of a great city
and the hush of all the ages,
a monument to that
which is always
moving, never ceasing—
and ever standing, still.

PERCEPTIONS

DELVING

"Now *that's* what I call
a tree," you said, as we turned
a corner, and came upon it
with a start.

Dark branches
stretching for the sky,
higher than the eye could see
as we stood beneath. But

it was the roots that took me:
knotted and veined, partly visible
and huge, each one thicker
than a human torso,

twisting over and around
each other to delve as deep
as they could dive
into the dirt of earth.

FIRST FLUSH

Not yet one day old and as we,
with your mother, stare, aching,
at the soft throb of your vulnerable
skull, your neck so soft, too slight, as yet,
to hold your head but already elegant, like hers;

as we gaze at your gossamer brows,
your crystalline skin, with wonder
last felt thirty years before, at your
tiny nails, each one of ten a pin-point
of pure perfection on your cupped feet and fingers

the sun comes out, emerging from clouds
we'd failed to notice until then.
And as through the window sunlight
passes for the first time, across your face,
with you we are each illuminated, all newborn.

EMIGRATION SONG

Moonlight over Slade Harbour.
Low tide. Four beached boats,
stranded, await the waves' return.
Something in their marooning

draws a gasp from me,
unaccountably. Then tears,

as if from nowhere, come.
Memory unlocked.
The pull of home.
The pity of it all.

We had to go, I know, I know.
The grounded boats agree.

Under their consoling gaze
and the clear regarding moon
I cry for what went
unmourned. What had to be.

And for the sweet new
knowing now delivered here.

We were not abandoned. No.
Only dry-docked awhile,
in our sorrow forgetting
the waves' inevitable return.

A REPLY AND AN ANSWER

Listen, my parents:
the grasses are crawling,
the trees are thrumming,
soon birds won't be able to sing.
Listen. Hear me. Our time is for turning.
If the old ways don't die, we can't win.

Listen, my children:
the grasses *are* crawling,
the trees *are* thrumming,
birds know what they know as they sing.
Listen. Hear it. True time ever calling.
Lay down your despairing, join in.

TURNING POINT

AN IRISH BLESSING

For Kathy

May you know many a moment when
the wind facing strongly into you
turns
to brace your back and lift your legs,
now bearing you along.

May you know many a moment when
the sun hidden behind hill and cloud
breaks
to let its rays light up your face,
now turning you warm.

May you know many a moment when
the road rising steep and stoney
crests
to a grass path turned towards your feet,
now urging you on.

May you know many a moment when

the rains falling hard on your forehead
lift
to fall soft and light on your heart,
now settling you down

here, where you may know many a moment
of comfort, holding the wind and the sun,
the road and the rain, and holding too
the knowing that each and all
were always turning you towards here
now, always taking you home.

CIRCLE OF LIFE

...again? Are you not mother? That
is the question that must be posed
and not just to those who
work the world with their pants
less stuffed, with their arms
held aloft, when not wrapped
round the chores and the children.

No, to the big boys too, those who sooner
or later come home crying over having
to do what they had to do. Yes Sirs,
also: same question to you.

It's not just the body that moulds
and anyhow the earth that births
the him and the her of it all shall,
in its time — own and good — make
a meal of our segments, slurp us up.

And, we presume,

be disappeared
in her turn.

Never fear. Know the question is all
that remains: how to birth? And how
to be born? Again? And again? And…

PLACENTA

Look to the tree,
how it remembers the clay
that once pressed, loam-loving,
round its kernel
through which it roamed
out, a tender and unseeing shoot,
groping towards
the light of day
and the airy, spangled light of night,

how it poked itself up,
thin and twiggy-green, dazzled
but drawn by the taste of wind,
the touch of sky,
to rise and rise.

Oh yes, sap soaring,
up it flew,
thickening to wood as it went,
circling its circles,
and pouring out leaves and fruit,

leaves and fruit, leaves and fruit,
to flare and fall,
year after year,
from its trunk.
One dear trunk,
so tall and split and spread,
fingering the air,
its strength its equal,
rooting reach for earth.

TAGUS: RIVER STORY

The river flows
as a river does
begetting
as a river must.
And begotten.

To us, drawing your line
on schoolgirl maps,
you were The Tay-gus, hard g.
Your own lands double-named you:
Tajo in Spain; in Portuguese
—that tongue I love
that shifts 's' sounds to shhh—
Taj-oosh.

Through our many mouths you flow
Tay-gus, Tagus, Tajo.
And from your source
through mountains and plains
to the sea city birthed by you: *Lisboa.*

On its banks, cruise ships dock in stops
along the bay, from Santa Apolónia
to Alcântara. Once, it was you who
sent out ships round the world,
cargoing six centuries of empire:
from the capture of Cueta
to the return of Macau.
The longest-lasting imperial power.

Now flamingos and dolphins play
in your waters, shallow and deep,
and tourists come to capture the castle,
the sea and the sun on their phones.
I am one. Here with five friends
who went to the school where
we learned to configure you
and the rest of our world.
Three of us know each other
since we were four, three more
since the start of our teens.
Now, we are here, on the cusp
of the decade said by the psalms
to crown the span of a life.
Almost three score. And still
coming together, year after year,
each time the returning more dear.

And the river flows
as a river does
begetting
as a river must.
And begotten.

At the tourist spot *Cristo-Rei,*
a Christ-the-King replica
of Rio's Christ-the-Redeemer
canonical chant comes from a speaker

in the church door. The biggest Jesus
we've ever seen concrete arms winged
over city and sea. Eighty-two meters
of plinth, 28 meters of a god said
to be twice-born. A man beyond
the facts of life, of death, of women.

The Tagus appears first in the mountains
of Spain, springing to surface not,
as long thought, at Fuente de Garcia
but six miles higher. Fuente de Juan Ribo
is now said to be the site of its source.
Up there, it cuts through limestone,
flows fast through red canyons and deep
brown ravines. As girls we wore
pinafores that precise shade of brown,
bright red ties round our necks,
sashes slashed round our waists.

Last night, at dinner, a man's face
loomed into our good times, bellyaching.
"I don't want to hear you," he shouted,
stopping our talk. We looked round.
Had we been loud? The staff apologised
to us for him. To him for us.
We wanted to leave but also to cleave
to our right to be here, to be heard.
The two ways of being in the world.

And the river flows
as a river does
begetting
as a river must.
And begotten.

Portugal had a unique revolution:
mutiny with barely a shot.

At the behest of a restaurant worker,
Celeste dos Cravos, the people
pushed carnation flowers
into the muzzles of guns,
ending the age of a dictator
and the long-lamented colonial war.
Revolution, Marx said, is a midwife,
new ways born from the old.
Who cares for what was birthed
by Celeste and her fiesta of flowers?

When the day comes that this city
is gone and only the stories remain,
will they tell only of Afonso or Sancho,
the crusaders and *reconquistas*,
the sea battles and sieges
gods and women made in the likeness
of men, all that's lasted into our days?

Never mind. We six are here,
come from all parts of the world
to be together and talking today.
The dolphins are leaping.
The flamingos stand on one claw.
A river is more than the sliver
we see. And lunch by the bayside
is waiting. Let's go. But let us know
that Tagus has washed her way through
the multi-hued earth of the mountains
and the overflow of the plains

to empty, in a tumult of joy at returning,
into the sea. Let us see how she
dances in the rays of the sun
splays open the mouth of the bay,
evaporates into the air, to be
carried back there to the mountains

in clouds full of sunshine and rain,
to dissolve into her bounty again.
Again. And again. And again.

For a river flows
as a river does
begetting
as a river must.
And begotten.

WHERE ARE YOU?

Where are you?
The splendor of creation awaits.
Beauty veiled, she dallies,
playing with the wings of birds passing,
swaying her hips
with the wind, wanting
to dance, to bring you music
from planets and clouds.

Call her by right name,
hear her answer.
Male or female,
she is yours:
lingering, singing and playing,
holding out a braceleted hand,
all tinkle and glint.
She wants to roll ecstasy
over and under your skin,
swirl bubblings into your blood,
breathe you away
through the waves of the ages.

You can stay where you are
(where are you?)
and just listen.
No, don't even listen, just be.
Unmask. That is all.
She will offer herself,
unasked and unasking.
No demands from her,
ever, to know: where are you?

ORAN MÓR

FROM THE IRISH CREATION MYTH

For Phil the Murph

Long before the coming
of the gods, or the giants,
before man or woman
stalked or walked,
in the space that came
before time,
before the ocean had
a wave in it, even,
it was the sea bed
that had the giving
of things, out of
the unending
silence of its open
underneath.

Up from there somehow
(no-one ever knew how
and don't worry yourself
no-ever will) up from

there, out of all
that was still,
came the first strain
of the the first note
that first shifted
the waters.

The first sounding
of the sounds
that would go on
to be known as
Oran Mór.
The great song.

When it came to the shore
the great silence
gave voice to the waves.
Only a whisper
when it began,
but louder it grew
and then surer,
circling into a
spiral, out and up,
gathering sound,
the music of
Oran Mór.
The great song.

Out of the sea-foam,
a sea-horse was born—
a mare, by the name
of Eiocha. Oran Mór
got a taste for it then
and many more came after,
sung out of the sound
that was singing itself
through the waters into

the land, one thing
begetting another until,
one day
from a great oak tree,
Eiocha sprouted
a plant and birthed
out of *Oran Mór*,
the great song
the first god.

Then when Eiocha hurled
a branch into the water,
giants too were born
from the bark of that tree,
and with the gods mated
and begot more gods
and more giants, who
learned how to hew
from the wood, how
to hoe from the water
how to be sung through
Oran Mór, the great song,
In delight, it sang on.

On it sings still
harmonizing all.
Woman and man.
Animal and plant.
Mineral and air.
Earth, sap and fire.
The moreness of more.
Oran Mór.
The great song.

EXTINCTION REBELLION?

I see the sun rise in the east,
over the waves, and am brought
to wonder at its endeavor.
Do you think we will ever know
what we should do with human trying?

How to forgive the plying of fear into flags
how to caress the fists of effort, open
them out and kiss the wrinkled palms
for needing too hard, for calling war?

How we might quiver into feeling
the rest of our being?

The neck as honored to lower as to lift.
The back made to bend or return to erect.
The arms that can splay as well as hug close.
The chest with its close encasement of ribs,
so open between and behind,
holding, without touching,
the lungs it exists to protect.

The diaphragm allowing the softness
of breath. The stomach digesting,
removing the waste. The pelvis,
its bowlful of organs and needs. The legs
that can run and fall to their knees.
The feet that can stop as sure as they stalk.

And the hands. Those twin hands
which can interlace fingers,
or spiral and twist,
both out on their wrists,
that can cup fistfuls of air to throw over hair
to fall flowing, or splash into a face
that knows how to smile,
into eyes that can own what they own,
into ears that can hear cries harmonizing
across tongues that tell longing in song,
along trunks that undulate dance out of howls,
through a being that knows how to belong.

I see the sun in the west, over land
receding, revealing all the other bodies
of light and wonder at that revelation.

Do you think we'll ever allow
moon and stars to lead us
into the kindness of dark?
Let the flags of the nations wave
gaily, without flapping the skin
and skulls of our sons? Know
the he-men who unpin the bombs
are also she-girls in the dark,
ashamed of what we need,
calling for mommy through dreams
of delivering imperfect ribbons of peace.

With each of us a devil divine

do you think we will ever call time
know which parts we must hold
with rejoicing,
which must be let go?
And how?
Bury our weapons
so deep they can't be recalled
except as low warning
of death ways long gone?

Hold gently the creatures
of the depths and the shores
and let them lead us
out of our charge towards the end
into what we could—still yet—become,
if we could only know how,
if we could but unfurl to allow?

COFFEE BREAK

A woman at the cafe table, age-quavering.
Cappuccino foam on her chin,
tributaries of wrinkles around her eyes
obscuring their flint.

She is struggling with her cup.
Big as a bowl, full to the brim,
too heavy for wrists so thin.

It slips and spills. With a sigh,
she submits, switches to spoon
and to lips that have eagerly opened
Lifts a trembling thimbleful ration.

And then: a lifetime's joy in good coffee
erupts in a glorious grin.
Up she sits to spoon again.

DAY'S END

There are days
that don't want to leave us.
Evening comes and they
put on their finery:
cloaks of gold
and amber
copper and rose
edged with flame
of aureate, burnishing
orange, the colors
of elements that last aeons
and hold back.

Dressed for departure,
they wait on the threshold,
languid, dazzling, fine,
like they have forever
tucked away
in their pockets and folds.

Though we both know

they must go,
they linger as long
as they can
before kissing us goodbye
with a final flash
of their cloak,
whispering
as they dip behind
the horizon:
"Though
we must leave,
please ensure
that we shall not
be forgotten."

THE LONG-MEMORIED SEA

Come in now, won't you?
Come in for a swim.
Come on in.

Today I'm soft turnings
kissing the land all along
its shoulder and arm
the full length of the sand

I know: that's how you like it. *Aaah...*

Forget the mad moods of midnight
the surfeit of watered-up wind
smashing your vessels
the crashing into the chest
the choking of lungs
that was a different time
so it was.

So it was.

Before there was air, I was here.
Off you went on your legs
telling your stories.
You never knew how to tell this.
Words, how are ya.

How are you?

I'm here, still,
so I am.

So I am.

All stillness
in my better part
in the back beyond
in the black beneath
fathoms afar
under the fallen

birthing the creatures of color
allowing the unheeding light.

Come in now.
Come on in.
Come in and swim.

RENOVATION

A scaffold round our house.
Two men scraping paint off brick,
releasing red dust everywhere.

We fear the neighbors must complain.
We'll have to pay to hose down
half the street when we complete.

On we go, though, scraping
and mending the mortar cracks
revealed, casting our paint-powder,
as we must, to the air, uncovering

what was unseen but always there,
solid beyond cement fissures:
the golden bricks, so bright,
so beautiful, beneath.

PRACTICE

FOLLOWINGS

Creatives grope through the dark
drawn by the promise of dawn
our way lit by the stars
who smile on our stumbles
know why we seek
and love what our searching creates.

WHATEVER

Whatever you do,
my dear maker,
don't go looking for yourself,
or seeking to improve.
You are not to be found,
and nothing whatever in you
needs to be fixed.

You, my beauty, are
what you are
and whatever you are
currently
creating from that.

Don't allow yourself
to be riven.

You don't need
to be political,
or intellectual.
Charitable

or emblematical.
You have no need to repent.
And no reason to revert.
The motion you seek
is one of release.

Relent. Say, in your own way
whatever it was
your ancestors meant
when they declared
god to be good.

And whatever you make
from the undulating being
you've been given,
make it loud. Do it proud.

MORNING PRACTICE

Dedicated to our morning practice group on Facebook Live.
Facebook.com/groups/
Go.Creative.Daily.Flow.Practice

Sit to silence
hear a singing,

in the silence
know the song.

Know the silence
is me singing,

by the silence
am I sung.

Sit to writing
In the silence

Through the writing
see the thought

See the silence
through me thinking

by the writing
am I wrought.

Sit to silence
hear a singing,

in the silence
know the song.

Know the silence
is me singing,

by the silence
am I sung.

UNDERSCORE

In the opening of morning
I go down to the ocean
to let thought come undone
in the waves' whoosh and turn.

From his perch on a stone
a long-haired young man
looks up from his guitar
continues to strum
as he gives me a grin,
that says I should sit down
on a stone of my own.

Above, on the prom
the runners have begun
and the early road traffic
is starting to drum.

Down here by the ocean
the tide's pressing in,

but with young music
man, I sit on. Our two faces
upturned, are deep warmed
by the sun and the sound
of the sea underscoring his song.

HUSH

Hush. Don't speak it aloud, beloved,

the crowd will sneer. Though

we know what we hold,

whisper it only to the wise

and to me, made wise by our love.

Take my hand from your mouth,

see, fade yours into mine. Feel

me here. And here. Dying.

Dying for you. Murmur wings

of gossamer steel into being,

wave their wind through

the turnings of time. Oh yes,

we will ruffle the shrouds, we

will upend the season's

parading if we only allow.

Come. Cup our breath,

our shared life,

two made one, into none.

Shade us out. Sigh it sheer.

FONT OF TRUTH

The truest words
are born in silence.
From well of quiet
springs font of truth.

Though blood may rage
and brain may clamor
and body blare
from head to root,

the deepest pulses
throb in whispers.
The still observing
soul stays mute.

I wish you all
the grace of silence
the quiet that's known
when speaking truth.

FLOW

I wish we could flow as oceans tide,

swelling with joy at our urge to unfurl.

I feel we should roll as planets turn,

dark days and seasons held level with light.

I sense we can grow as mountains rise

from stresses rock setting, solid and free.

I intend to go as children run,

arms wide, smile plunging, into full stop.

ALLOWING NOW

WITH THANKS TO ECKHART TOLLE

The talkers talk
of leaving
or remaining
who should go,
what cannot stay,
who's right,
what's wrong,
where's goodness gone?
Too many old,
the lawless young,
we're bound to pay,
we'll come undone,
the planet's doomed,
the coming bomb.

No. I'll feed no more
on skeletons of gloom
and ruin. Death knells
of what the world calls
news, filtered through
someone else's blues.

I close my ears
to third-hand tales.
I breathe my breath:
Inhale. Exhale.

Buoyed in the surge of now
washed in the flow of now
swirled in the swell of now
lulled in the well of now

I find perception magnified.
I see the world with different sight.

Our young, who never flourished more
than they now grow
our old, who never garnered more
than they now know.

Peace, never more feasible
than now
happiness, never more possible
than now
knowledge never more accessible
than now
All we know as goodness
never more reachable than now.
And goodness knows
no matter what
our human selves decide
to think or do
life comes in peace
and we are all as welcome
as we ever were, here,
in the holy, flowing hold of now.

THE END

ACKNOWLEDGMENTS

My thanks to Jane Dixon Smith for her fabulous cover art and design, to Sarah Begley, for publishing assistance, and to Philip Lynch for early readings.

Thanks especially to my patrons on Patreon, who keep me connected to poetry when other demands try to haul me away. Knowing you're there, offering my poems such direct support on Patreon, really helps and I'm fiercely grateful. Thank you for your monetary support but also your time and attention and for empowering me to follow my vocation as well as my avocation.

With a bow, thank you. *Namaste! Sonas!*

FREE BOOK & AUDIOBOOK

SELECTED POETRY FOR SUBSCRIBERS

Send me your email address and I'll forward you a free ebook of **Selected Poetry**—together with an audiobook of me reading the poems?

CLICK HERE TO SIGN UP FOR AN EBOOK AND AUDIO DOWNLOAD

I'll also send you my monthly poetry news and information about the Self-Publishing Poetry Podcast.

MORE POETRY

I also have a poetry page on Patreon, with dedicated poems, signed books and other gifts and giveaways each month, exclusively for my patrons, who help me to keep the poems coming.

There's a special reward tier for other poets.

Do join me in this exclusive space for poets and poetry lovers.

www.patreon.com/ornaross

Allowing Now
Selected Inspirational Poetry

© Orna Ross 2019

978-1-913349-10-3 ebook
978-1-913349-11-0 -paperback
978-1-913349-12-7 hardback
978-1-913349-13-4 large print
978-1-913349-14-1 audio

ALL ENQUIRIES: INFO@ORNAROSS.COM

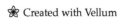 Created with Vellum

I WOULD LOVE YOUR FEEDBACK

REVIEW REQUEST

If you enjoyed this book, would you consider leaving a brief review online on Goodreads, your website or other favorite online bookstore?

A good review is very important to authors these days as it helps other readers know this is a book worth their time.

It doesn't have to be long or detailed. Just a sentence saying what you enjoyed and a star-rating is all that's needed.

A shoutout on social media or on the guestbook on my website is also greatly appreciated .

Please accept my thanks, in advance, if this is something you'd like to do.

Review on Amazon
or your preferred online store

Font Publications is the publishing imprint
for Orna Ross, the Creativist Club
and the Alliance of Independent Authors.

All Font books—fiction, non-fiction and poetry—have the same intention at source: to
inspire creative independence, emotional freedom and imaginative connection.
All Enquiries: info@ornaross.com

"To go creative return to the font."